WISE Women Empower Women

Stories of Women Who Embody the Spirit of the Proverbs 31 Woman

Jennifer Sanchez

WISE Women Empower Women: *Stories of Women Who Embody the Spirit of the Proverbs 31 Woman*

ISBN: 979-8-218-94999-0

The scriptures mentioned within this journal can be found in the

New King James Version and the Message Bibles.

Publisher: VOS Consulting and Publishing International

E: hello@yourauthorsauthority.com

W: yourauthorsauthority.com

Editor: Alan Black

E: hello@yourauthorsauthority.com

Acknowledgments

I want to take a moment to recognize all the women featured in this book, as well as their families, for supporting them throughout this journey. I would also like to thank the publisher and her team for helping bring this book to life. I am deeply grateful to the women in my community and to my daughters for their inspiration and encouragement in making this book possible.

I'd like to extend a special thank you to Carlos Medina of Medina Visual Productions, along with Alex Salazar, my videographer, and Mario Jimenez, my photographer. Your work truly helped bring this vision to life.

To my interns and students from Illinois Media School, thanks for everything. To my spiritual mom Nancye F. Rivera, thank you for your love and support in my faith journey. To my parents and sister, thanks for believing in me and being my rock during the difficult times of my life.

Finally, I thank God for planting this seed in me years ago and for continuing to guide me in my work of supporting women.

Table of Contents

Letter to The Readers

Dear Readers,

I want to express my sincere gratitude to you, the reader, for supporting the women featured in this book. One of the most empowering things a person can do in their lifetime is put their story on paper and share it with the world. It is also one of the most intimidating, as it requires vulnerability and the courage to reveal parts of life that may have long been hidden. This has been a deeply healing experience for each of these women, and it is also a reflection of the years of work I have devoted to WISE, (Women's Institute of Self Development & Efficacy). My greatest joy as the visionary of this book is empowering women. The women who shared their stories here worked diligently to bring their experiences to light, and it has been an honor to encourage and walk alongside them on a weekly basis. One of my greatest accomplishments is bringing this body of work together in a way that glorifies God. Truly, my life's work is represented in these pages, and I pray you recognize that what you hold is a piece of my heart.

When God first called me to serve women, I wanted to run from it. Much like Jonah and the whale, He continued to call me back. Now, nearly a decade later, I see God's hand moving not only in my life, but in the lives of the women I have served and their families. I firmly believe that when you help one woman live a healthier, happier life—and show her that she is a ruby—she becomes an asset to her family. Women are catalysts for change within their homes. I truly believe these women will go on to do amazing things and God gets all the glory. At the end of the day, this is all God's work, and we are simply vessels to carry out His will. I also hope that this book brings you closer to God. I don't know where you are in your life, but it's possible that this book did not come into your hands by coincidence—it may be a God-incidence. I don't know what you are going through, but my prayer is that as you read these stories, you will feel God's presence and hear His gentle whispers speaking to your heart. The greatest gift I can offer you is the opportunity to receive God as your Lord and Savior. My life was transformed when I chose to follow Him. It hasn't been easy, but I would never choose a life without Him. After reading this book, if you feel led to accept Jesus as your Lord and Savior, there is a salvation prayer at the end of the book.

As you read it, I encourage you to make it personal.

Jennifer Sanchez

Foreward

There are moments in life when words feel too small to capture the goodness of God.

And yet... here we are.

This book is not just a collection of stories—it is a living, breathing testimony of what happens when God steps into broken places and makes them whole. Each woman within these pages carries a story marked by trials, transitions, and transformation. And through it all, one truth remains: God has been good. I know this not just as an observer—but as a witness in my own life.

There was a time when my heart was heavy with wounds I didn't know how to name. Church hurt left me questioning what I once believed. Domestic violence tried to silence my voice. The absence of my father created a void that shaped how I saw myself, my worth, and the love I thought I deserved.

I was searching... for validation, for identity, for something to fill the emptiness.

At just 14 years old, I made a decision that was rooted in that longing—a longing to feel seen, valued, and loved. Without the guidance of a father's presence, I didn't yet understand the fullness of who I was or whose I was.

But even then… God saw me.

Through every broken place, every moment of confusion, every decision made out of pain—He never left me.

There were times my life could have ended. Moments where darkness felt louder than purpose. Even as I approached 30, after a tragic accident that shook my life to its core, the enemy whispered lies, trying to convince me that my story was over… that my life was no longer worth living.

But God.

God stepped in with grace when I didn't deserve it, with mercy when I didn't understand it, and with love that refused to let me go.

He healed my heart.

He restored my identity.

He reminded me that I was never abandoned…even when it felt like I was.

What the enemy meant for destruction, God used for revelation. He showed me that my story was never meant to end in pain—but to be transformed into purpose.

And that is what this book represents.

These stories are not about perfection. They are about redemption.

They are not about having it all together. They are about surrender.

They are not about where we started—but about the God who carried us through.

If you are reading this and find yourself in a place of hurt, confusion, or searching... I want you to know this:

God sees you.

God knows you.

And God is not finished with you.

Let these pages remind you that no matter what you've faced, no matter what you've lost, no matter what you've been told—your story still holds power.

Because when God steps in... everything changes.

And just like He did it for me, and for the women in this book—

He can do it for you.

In His Love,

Dr. Toccara Nicole

CHAPTER 1

I Couldn't Hear, Because I Wasn't Listening

Angel Robledo

"Codependency is a relationship pattern where a person becomes emotionally dependent on someone else for their sense of worth, identity, and stability, often by putting the other person's needs far above their own."

I never thought God spoke to me the way I would hear others say He spoke to them. I'd heard people say God whispers to them or speaks to them when they needed it most. Some say they actually hear His voice. But I never felt that. I never heard a whisper. I never heard a voice speaking directly to me.

For many years, I felt that God didn't really care about me at all. I went about my life, living for myself. I didn't pray, and I didn't go to church. I did go to a Catholic High School. I received all my sacraments. I just never felt connected to God. I know all the prayers; The Our Father, The Hail Mary, in English and in Spanish, but still I never felt close to Him.

I received my first communion at about 11 years old. I was one of the oldest kids in my catechism class. I hated being there, but my parents made me go. In my mind, I was there for them. I didn't want any part of it, but I did it because that's what they expected of me. Looking back, I'm sure there are many kids that feel this way. Shortly after that, I found out my parents were divorcing. How could they want me to be religious but planning a divorce all at the same time.

To me, God felt farther away than ever.

Much of the memories of the time from finding out my parents were getting divorced to actually experiencing the separation are a blur. I've learned that losing memories like that can be a trauma response. At that time, I felt like my life was just pointless. I struggled a lot after my parents separated. It was kinda like the adults in the room had forgotten all about the kids; my brother (8) and me (12). The life I thought I had was all a lie. Suddenly the happy family I believed I belonged to no longer existed.

My brother and I went to live with our dad. He was distraught, and our lives were upside-down. I remember my grandmother (my mom's mom) once hiding us from our mom. She loved my dad so much and was upset at my mom for wanting the divorce. It was all so weird. Thinking back, it was like we were living in a movie. I remember my grandmother rushing us in her car and racing off quickly. My mom followed behind us in her car. It was like a high speed chase, and we were being kidnapped but it was my grandma and we were not in any harm. I remember my grandma asking if we could still see her behind us. She was trying to lose her. It was so strange, confusing and so weird.

Life was just not ideal for the soon-to-be teen, Angelica. But I felt safe because I was with my dad. He was always my hero.

...Until he wasn't.

He quickly fell into depression and was no longer the father figure that would take us for long bike rides or spend time gardening with us in the backyard or teaching us to make the delicious meals he would always cook. He turned into a broken man who had the carpet ripped from under him.

How could I believe God was with me?

As I reflect, I realize depression has been a part of my life for decades, whether it was mine or my father's.

During my teen years, God felt even farther. I searched for comfort in boys. I was the prime example of what it meant for someone to have "Daddy Issues." I had boyfriend after boyfriend. I never was without.

I got pregnant at sixteen. I had an abortion. My boyfriend left me shortly after. I felt broken, unloved, and worthless.

I barely graduated high school. I skipped school all the time. I didn't have many friends. Life was just passing me by and I was being dragged along.... That's what life felt like.

In my junior year of high school, I met another boy and he became the father to my first child at twenty years old. It was tough. But I finally thought something was going right when I had a beautiful baby girl on that beautiful April morning. I was finally starting to feel like something in my life was right.

For a while, I was happy.

Then that relationship fell apart. We separated less than 4 years after my daughter was born and the emptiness began to settle in once again. Instead of healing my "Daddy Issues," I once again ran straight into another relationship. I avoided the innerwork necessary. The work every person needs to do when ending a life changing chapter of their lives.

And I became pregnant again.

In what felt like an instant, I had another "family", a new partner and two children. But the emptiness inside me was overwhelming and overbearing. I looked to this new partner to help me feel loved, valued, and feel important. I never did.

Now I know that this was co-dependency.

According to AI, codependency is a relationship pattern where a person becomes emotionally dependent on someone else for their sense of worth, identity, and stability—often by putting the other person's needs far above their own. That was me. I searched for my worth in men who could never love me the way Jesus loves me.

My son was born in 2006. Shortly after, I lost my job. I developed postpartum depression. I felt trapped in an unhealthy, co-dependent relationship.

I felt I was never enough. I felt unloved and worthless yet again. On September 16, 2007, I attempted suicide for the first time. It was my brother's wedding day. It was after an argument with my son's father. He was at work. I believe my kids went to the party with my mother. I was home alone. All I remember was waking up on the bathroom floor by my son's father shoving his fingers down my throat to make me throw up. I had taken a lot of Tylenol. I don't remember how many but at the time, I said to myself I didn't take enough.

I didn't go to the hospital. No one took me. No one insisted.

Years later, in 2010, I reached another breaking point.

My depression continued. Life continued reminding me everyday that I was not enough, that I was unloved, that I never did anything right. I was having suicidal thoughts once again.

One cold, rainy afternoon, I walked two miles to the nearest hospital in my pajamas and socks. No shoes. No plan, just desperation and fear. Fear I would try to kill myself again. I told the hospital staff. I was honest and transparent. I told them everything; that it wasn't the first time, that I actually tried once before and failed, that I needed help, and that I wanted help. I was sick and tired of being sick and tired.

I was admitted for a week.

A therapist was assigned post-visit. I learned new coping skills and identifiers of my triggers. I learned that I need to ask for help when I need it. I learned that no one is perfect. I learned I needed to stand up for myself more, and I needed to take more time for me to find happiness outside of my relationship; that I was more than a "wife" and a mom. This is when I learned I was co-dependent. I learned that I was in an unhealthy relationship. I learned I needed anti-depressants. In some ways the anti-depressants made me even more depressed. I gained weight. My libido was down. I was hormonal. I was irritable and argued with the people in my life more than before.

Something was still missing.

In January 2011, I tried again. I took half a bottle of Lexapro, the anti-depressants the doctor had me on. I vaguely remember what happened as I was in-and-out of consciousness but I do remember hospital staff commenting on the fact that it was ironic how I would choose to take the anti-depressant that was supposed to help me feel better to "off" myself. The shame settled in and a feeling of inadequacy came over me. I thought to myself, I can't even do this right, and now everyone is making fun of me. Depression was a black cloud and it was raining only on me.

This time I didn't have medical insurance so when I was hospitalized, I was sent to a state mental health facility. It was terrifying at first. It was nothing like the first time I was admitted. At this facility, I found myself on the same floor as people struggling with BPD, schizophrenia, OCD, and other mental health challenges. I didn't know when they were going to release me, but as the days went on and I remained in that place, I found myself getting comfortable and an unexpected peace.

I realized I needed something more than therapy and medication. I needed peace. Shortly after being released I confided in a new friend. I told her that I felt lost, alone, defeated. I told her my story. She told me I needed Jesus. She asked me if I belonged to a church. I did not. I hadn't even thought about God anymore. I knew of him. I knew about him, but never did I think Jesus was what was missing. I didn't know what that meant but I was at my wits end. I was tired of being tired. She invited me to New Life Community Church.

A Christian Church felt so strange to me at first; everyone was singing loudly, the full band, the idea of "come as you are", but most of all the overwhelming feeling I had every time I was there. The message would hit my heart like a dagger.

I found myself sobbing uncontrollably but in a good way every time I was there. I longed for a connection with God for so long. I felt it there. I can't find any other explanation for it. I felt calm. I felt I belonged even when I knew no one. I found peace.

I slowly began to learn that God was always whispering to me.

He was whispering to me every time I attempted to end my life. A feeling of "why did I just do that?" would always come over me after. I believe God was convicting me at the moment. When I thought it was all over, he whispered to me, "I'm not done yet". When my partner found me in time to make me vomit the pills I had swallowed, he whispered to me, "not today". When my barefoot steps took me to that emergency Room, he whispered to me, "let's go for a walk". When my son's father took me to the hospital that third time, he whispered to me, "not this time". He never left me.

God allowed things to happen because I chose to put myself in situations he never even wanted for me. He gave us free will, but He is always there. It was my fear and insecurities that kept me in a relationship that was destroying me. He was always speaking to me, the problem was that I wasn't listening. I wasn't seeking him. I wasn't aligned with him. Once I made God the center of my life, the anxiety fled, the sadness fled, the self-judgement fled.

Loving God became my therapy. God's love became my medicine. I learned it's okay to find refuge in him even when I'm not perfect nor have everything all together. See God loves us with all our flaws and insecurities. He is the Father I always needed. He loves me more than I could ever imagine. I never really understood it until I searched for him. I never really felt it until I learned more about who he is and what he's done for me, and YOU.

Loving God and drawing near to him in daily conversation (prayer) has been medicine that saved my life.

Reflection:

What comes to mind when you think of God being your medicine?

What coping skills do you use when things get tough in your life?

When you hear "drawing closer to God," what comes to mind?

About the Author

Angel Robledo is a Chicago native and small business owner, she is a devoted mother to two children, Monica and Omar Isaiah, and the creative force behind her custom cake business. Her journey has been shaped by faith, personal growth, and the resilience built through life's challenges.

As a co-author in a faith-based book, she shares her story with honesty and heart, using her voice to inspire healing, connection, and a deeper relationship with God. Her writing is raw, relatable, and conversational, reflecting her belief that there is power in being seen, heard, and understood.

Through both her writing and her work, she hopes to remind others that they are never alone, always loved, and continually covered by God's grace.

CHAPTER 2

The Love I Always Searched For

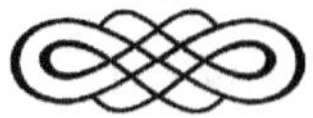

Maria Solis

"The love of God cannot be compared to anything else.

It is a love that does not demand, does not fail, and does not depend on conditions in order to exist."

Dedication to God, who lifted me when I no longer had the strength to stand. To my mother, my father, and my grandmother for their unwavering faith and their prayers that brought me back home. And to every person who needs to remember that no matter their past, God can make everything new with His love.

Before I Knew True Love

From a very young age, I searched for love, approval, and identity in the wrong places without realizing that God had always been there. For many years I felt inadequate and carried the constant feeling that nothing I did was ever enough or truly right.

The wounds that began in my childhood followed me silently into adulthood. From a very early age, I learned what it felt like to be alone. I remember the rejection I sometimes felt for being different, for not fitting in, or for being a quiet and reserved girl who carefully measured her words and actions out of fear of bothering or disappointing others.

Although it was difficult for me to approach people or even begin a conversation, deep inside I always wanted to. Fear was simply stronger. I longed to feel acceptance, belonging, and affection, yet the fear of rejection held me back. Despite my insecurities, I always tried to act with love. I never carried hatred or resentment toward anyone. I simply learned to step away so I would not continue hurting myself.

I always knew that God existed, although I did not truly know Him. Over time I began to understand that His presence had been with me all along, even in my silence and in my tears. Today I understand that the love of God cannot be compared to anything else.

It is a love that does not demand, does not fail, and does not depend on conditions in order to exist. Once I came to know that love, I stopped searching for acceptance from others. I realized that human love can fail, but the love of God is perfect and unconditional.

The Little Girl Who Wanted to Be Enough

From a very young age I longed to be closer to my mother. I loved her deeply, but I often felt a certain distance between us. It was not a lack of love. She simply carried a very heavy burden. My father worked in the United States and visited whenever he could. During that time my mother took on the responsibility of being both mother and father. Now I understand that this was not easy for her, and I know she did more than she possibly could, even though I did not understand it then.

Thank God I did not grow up lacking material things. Because of my parents' sacrifices, we always had a roof over our heads and food on the table. Yet the soul also feels hunger, and mine longed for affection, love, time, and hugs. My father once taught me something I will never forget. He said, “Not with blows.” With those words he showed me that respect is not born from fear. Even though his work kept him far away, his example stayed with me because it was not only his words but also the way he lived.

As a child I dreamed of having a warm home with my parents. Every time my father had to return to the United States, watching him board the airplane broke my heart. I cried and screamed, wishing I could go with him without fully understanding that the distance he endured was also an act of love and sacrifice for our family.

The year 2000 became a turning point in my life. I remember praying with all my heart and asking God to take me to be with my father. Day after day I prayed with the pure faith and hope of a child. In His immense love, God heard my prayers. In March of that same year my life changed completely. My mother, my siblings, and I left our country to go live with my father in the United States. It was the beginning of a new stage filled with emotions, challenges, and change.

Adapting was not easy. School was difficult and I experienced rejection because I suffered from bullying. I often felt out of place. Yet seeing my father every day gave me the strength to endure it all. For the first time I felt that our family was whole and that love was complete. Even though I did not fully understand it then, God was already working in my life.

My Definition of Love

Even after my family was reunited, something still felt missing within me. A deep emptiness followed me everywhere, and nothing seemed able to fill it. Eventually I made the decision to leave my parents' home and form my own family. It was a sudden decision that came from my desire to feel loved. I believed I had found the person with whom I would share my life. However, neither of us was prepared for what a healthy relationship required.

I was searching for love, and he did not know how to give it. I tried hard to keep the relationship alive, hoping for gestures and kind words that never came. I loved him, but in the process I hurt myself. Over time my heart stopped believing that true love even existed.

Years later I met someone else who wrote me romantic letters filled with beautiful words. At first I did not believe them. In fact, I once tore up one of his letters. Yet he insisted so many times that I began to wonder if perhaps someone really could love me. In the end that relationship also brought pain. I realized that what he offered was not true love and that it did not come from God.

Eventually I reached my lowest point. I cried, asked for forgiveness, and felt completely empty. I tried to hold on to something that was not real until I understood that the only love that had never failed me was the love of God.

I had to reach my lowest moment before I could finally look up. In my despair I attempted to end my life by taking a bottle full of pills because I did not have the courage to try anything else. By the grace of God I did not succeed, but the damage to my health remained and the consequences are something I continue to live with today.

In that moment my soul surrendered. Yet in my brokenness I discovered something powerful. God loved me even in my darkest moment, and His love did not require me to be perfect. That day only God was with me, and if it had not been for Him I might not be here telling my story today.

My entire life I struggled with the idea of love. What I did not realize was that God was simply waiting for me to allow myself to be loved by Him. When I finally did, that love transformed my life completely.

The Emptiness Only God Could Fill

It was because of my mother, my father, and my grandmother that I returned to the path of God. They never stopped praying for me, and their prayers eventually bore fruit. Because of them, I am here today. For a long time, I believed that I had grown up lacking my parents' love. Yet in the end they were the ones who taught me the true meaning of forgiveness. One day my mother looked into my eyes and said something that changed me forever. She said, "No one is born knowing how to be a parent."

Those words restored something deep within my heart because they came from the sincerity of her soul. Over time I realized that my mother also carried wounds from her own childhood. As she came to know the love of God, she too began learning how to love in a new way. Together we began to heal.

Out of love I chose to walk away from everything that was hurting me. I decided to heal my heart through the love of God because I no longer wanted to live in sadness or bitterness. Slowly I began to experience a different kind of love. It was patient, gentle, and true. For the first time in my life I felt peace.

God became my refuge and the love that filled the empty spaces inside me. Little by little the emptiness in my heart began to disappear. Today I can say that I am a woman who is alive and renewed by His grace.

I am grateful for every person God has placed in my life along the way because through them I learned that His love is often revealed in the smallest gestures. The love of God is so powerful that there is no wound it cannot heal. He rescued me, transformed me, and taught me that His love is the only love truly worth having and the only love that remains.

The Love That Remains

No matter how painful your past may be, no matter what you have gone through or how many times you have fallen, God can make everything new through His unconditional love.

If you are walking through a difficult season today, remember this. The love of God is waiting for you with open arms. He asks nothing in return. He does not judge you, and He will never abandon you. His love does not depend on what you have done but on who you are. You are His daughter, His creation, and His treasure.

Life does not end when the world fails to offer you love. Life truly begins when you discover that the love of God is greater than any wound. I have experienced this truth myself, and I believe you can experience it too. God made me a new person through His love, and I know He can do the same for you if you simply have faith.

Reflection:

What is love to you?

How has God fulfilled your life?

How has your childhood influenced your life?

About the Author

Maria Solis is a first-time author and passionate storyteller. She writes from the heart to inspire healing, faith, and self-love. Born in Aguascalientes, Mexico, and now based in the United States, her journey is deeply rooted in resilience, personal growth, and her relationship with God. A proud mother of three, she draws strength and purpose from her children, who are her greatest motivation.

Her writing is emotional, honest, and grounded in real-life experiences, exploring themes of healing, transformation, and hope. Through her work, she seeks to connect with women navigating pain, encouraging them to rediscover their strength, embrace self-love, and trust in new beginnings.

CHAPTER 3

God Seeks You!

Amell Feliz

"God's will is not what we desire when we have not consulted with God for guidance."

The parable of the Shepherd leaving ninety-nine to search for the one lost sheep. Luke 15:4-7 (NIV)

Chest pounding, body uncomfortable, hands fidgeting as the pastor began the altar call was my first experiencing the Lord. I was around 9 years old, when these experiences at church started to happen. These encounters made me feel so uneasy that I avoided going to church with my family so that I wouldn't feel nervous during the altar call. I was around tons of family, aunts, uncles, cousins yet I did not feel comfortable sharing this experience with anyone.

Loneliness was a constant feeling for me when I was younger. I internalized processing feelings to be a non-existent activity that we did not have time for. I understood early on that my mom came to this country to give me opportunities that she did not have. This translated to being hyper focused on academics to become a professional. Although my mom and I were together all the time, there was still a disconnect between the two of us. I needed warmth from her, but she could not give me that, while working constantly to keep us afloat. I remember her being annoyed most days by the tiredness which meant staying in my room, doing my homework and not making much noise. Little did I know that I was learning to suppress emotions.

I continued the course with the millennial blueprint, doing good in school to get a good job which will lead to a good life. During my high school years, I was attracted to sports and school clubs (I joined everything from debate clubs to dance), these experiences helped me get out of my comfort zone and show up for myself. Then college opened my eyes to the possibilities of what a great career can look like for a young Latina like me. I knew I had to put myself in places to learn and connect with others. It was not until I reached my master's program that I started to struggle with imposter syndrome. At the same time as me starting the program, I got married.

Up until this point, my focus had been my professional endeavors with some personal development sprinkled here and there. Cue the entrance of the biggest personal development stage of all time, marriage. Two young people with a lot of dreams in their backpack along with a lot of unresolved blind spots. Conflicts began to show up because we were no longer in a loving bubble that neither of us could do anything wrong. My biggest issue was taking everything as a personal attack, which led to deep negative self-thoughts. I wanted his validation that I was worthy but I was not emotionally mature to express these feelings. I felt like the more I did to be a "good wife" was always overlooked by the things that were done wrong in the eyes of my husband.

My constant thoughts were, " I am not good enough", "Will I ever get this wife thing down", "What is wrong with me?" And the list went on during spiraling moments. As a result of this, my mind was in shambles. I couldn't get myself to live in the present moment, it was filled with sadness and this overwhelming weight that I couldn't shake. I did the next best thing; I knew what to do up to this point - to learn. I buried myself in personal development from all angles. I started to read books, find podcasts, therapy, and different courses to help me learn how to navigate what I was feeling in my marriage. I was going to fix myself to show up differently to my marriage.

In one of many programs I enrolled in, I met a dearest friend, who introduced me to the God that I had always believed in, but I did not walk with. I learned about reading scripture, fasting, praying strategically, and allowing God to speak. I finally understood God's role in our lives and that I needed Him above all. I gave my life to Jesus. I continued my walk as a believer. I felt like I was making progress towards my own self-belief and old narratives that no longer served me. 2020 rolled around changing everyone's life forever including mine. Again, our marriage was hit with another low, this was the turning point in my relationship with God.

How are we here again? Aren't I praying for marriage, doing the best I can to become a better person/wife. Life didn't seem fair, I did what I thought I was supposed to, yet I did not get the result I was expecting. I was angry at God. I stopped all personal development. I could not hear one more person say, to have faith and work on yourself. I felt defeated and I did not want to do anything to feel otherwise. I wore these feelings with pride, like I had reasons to be angry and that was that. I am extremely thankful for my friendships; they sat with me while I grieved what I couldn't put words to. They prayed and loved me when I felt like I had nothing else to give.

Months went by and I knew it was my friend's prayers, that I slowly started using my bible app. Then I went on to ask God to reveal to me what I needed to learn from this difficult time in my life. A lot of times we get so angry and act like our situations are God's fault, as if we did not make decisions without His guidance.

The answer was clear a few months later - my heart posture and erroneous thinking. I was focused on actions that I never consulted God on; I was performing to be a "good person". Which leads to the worldly thought that good things happen to good people. I believed I was a good person, yet my circumstances weren't changing. One day as I opened my bible to spend time with God, He took me to Romans 3. As it is written: "There is no one righteous, not even one; There is no one who understands; there is no one who seeks God. All have turned away, they have together become worthless; there is no one who does good, not even one. Romans 3: 9-12 NIV.

The main message of Romans 3 is that all humanity is sinful and has fallen short of God's glory, unable to be justified by their own works or the Law, but God provides a way for righteousness through faith in Jesus Christ's atoning sacrifice and making salvation a gift for all who believe.

This message changed my perspective on what it meant to follow Jesus. God does not work if you act a certain way, He can't be manipulated by your actions when your heart is not pure.

My actions were performative to get what I wanted from God. I was viewing my relationship with God as a transaction and not a relationship from pure intention that will produce fruit in due time. More importantly, God's will is not what we desire when we have not consulted with God for guidance. Jeremiah 17:9 states, "The heart is deceitful above all things and beyond cure. Who can understand it?" (NIV). Hence our relationship with God needs to be our priority and desire to grow in our walk with God. I found myself when I understood this concept. His goodness is always running after us. We just need to stop and receive it.

The next few months, I felt so ashamed for allowing myself to get to a point of not talking to God and asking Him to help me. I should've known better, how did I let this deter my walk with the Lord? I let the devil play with my thoughts and I felt my feelings were justified because life was not fair.

Here is the thing, God never told me to do all those things, I created this checklist of things to do. I was focused on changing a situation that required deeper work within myself that no podcast or conference was going to help. Only God. I asked God for forgiveness, to help me clean my heart so that I can serve him with a pure heart.

He took my deepest pain and turned it into good for His glory. He never left me and stood by me when I didn't deserve it. That is our God. Faithful and loving. He started working in my heart and removing idols that had no business being there. I had made my husband and my marriage my idols. I desired my husband's validation to feel worthy and marriage gave me purpose/status.

I had fallen into the trap of idolatry, desiring validation and purpose from things that are not God. Exodus 20:3-5: "You shall have no other gods before me. You shall not make for yourself a carved image... you shall not bow down to them or serve them". Idols can be people, status, things, anything that takes God's place in your heart. If this idea of idols makes you ponder if you have any idols, ask yourself two questions:

What do I spend most of my day thinking about? If God were to remove this from my life, will I be okay with that? Take time to answer those two questions during your time with God this week and ask God to reveal to you anything that does not belong in your heart.

I couldn't believe that, I had been on my walk with the Lord for about quite some time now and my issue was idolatry. Unfortunately, this happens more than we like to admit in the Christian community. We see people attend church for years and call out to God, yet their hearts are filled with unforgiveness, hurt, and idols. Let's not forget what Matthew 7:21-23 (NIV) warns, that not everyone claiming to follow Jesus ("Lord, Lord") will enter heaven, only those doing the Father's will. Repenting and truly seeking God's heart has made me whole, I no longer feel like something is missing in my life because I have the almighty's presence all around me.

If you are struggling with the same things repeatedly, it is time to ask for forgiveness and seek God with all your heart. Not the God others say, but the God that loves YOU and is willing to search for you when you have lost your way. Experiencing God for yourself is the ultimate blessing in our lives. God had put his eyes on me at a young age, but I did not have the language or understanding of his seeking for me. It took years before I could understand His place in my life, but every heartache has made the joy I feel from the Lord worth it. Let this show you that God is still not done with you. He is waiting for you to call out to Him and allow him to heal and restore your situation. You might not want to hear the truth but know that God's intention for your life is to prosper you and make you whole.

Prayer:

Lord, I know that you have left 99 for the 1, we turn to you to ask for your forgiveness for our transgressions. I believe you are the light and the truth. I pray that you open the hearts and ears of those reading this story and remind them how much you love them. I pray that they seek you to find themselves.

In Jesus Name, Amen.

Reflection:

Have you experienced loneliness and shamefulness? How does it feel? How do you overcome it?

What makes your life good enough?

How have you experienced God for yourself?

About the Author

Amell Feliz, is a Senior Operations Manager with over 15 years of experience at Staffmark, she has grown through multiple leadership roles and currently leads a team of five. She also serves as Chair of the company's Latin Business Resource Group and has been a dedicated coach with WISE since 2019, supporting workshops, retreats, and mentorship programs.

Originally from the Dominican Republic and now based in Chicago, she is a wife and mother of two who is deeply passionate about faith, personal growth, and helping others feel seen and supported. Although she never planned to become an author, she answered a call to share her journey with God, inspiring others, especially women, to recognize His presence in their lives and know they are never alone.

With a calm and heartfelt voice, she writes to encourage readers to reconnect with their faith, find purpose, and embrace the fullness of God's Kingdom.

CHAPTER 4

Chosen, Cherished, and Pursued

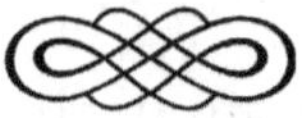

Vanessa Martinez-Torres

"You cannot out-love someone's free will. God Himself does not force transformation. He draws. He convicts. He corrects."

I remember the sound of my own crying. It was loud. Uncontrolled. Feral. The kind of crying that doesn't ask for permission and doesn't care who hears it. I was on the floor. My body trembling in waves I couldn't calm, my chest tight, breath so rapid you'd think I wasn't getting enough air. Hands shaking like they didn't belong to me anymore. Anxiety had taken over my nervous system. Something I couldn't talk myself out of. I had lost control.

I wasn't just sad. I was unraveling. I cried until my throat hurt. Until my eyes burned. Until my body felt emptied from stress induced vomiting. Even then, my heart still felt heavy. There was no strength, just desperation. I had reached the kind of breaking point where pretending was no longer possible. I had to face my emotions, face my truth, the one that I had been avoiding.

I crawled to my standing mirror, my knees pressed into the carpet, palms shaking as I pulled myself upright against the glass. The person staring back at me wasn't who I expected. It wasn't the adult who knew better. It wasn't the strong one everyone else saw. It was little me. Eyes searching. Holding her breath, bracing herself to see if this time she would be met or dismissed. She needed to be embraced instead of abandoned. Spoken to instead of met with silence. Chosen instead of tolerated.

I pressed my hand to the mirror and felt the ache rise in my chest, the kind that had been there long before the heartbreak of the relationship that just ended. And that's when It was revealed to me, I hadn't been fighting for love. I had been fighting for safety. I felt a deep sensation of overwhelming love fill my chest. I came closer, my forehead rested against the glass, breath fogging the surface as my arms wrapped around the mirror. The reflection moved with me, same trembling shoulders, and we let out the loud ache that would bring relief.

I held her there. Not rushing. Not pulling away. Not telling her to be strong. For the first time, I didn't leave. I didn't step back to distract myself. I didn't look away because it hurt too much. I stayed. I then wrapped my arms tightly across my own body like they were making a promise my body had been waiting to feel. "I'm not abandoning you. I'm not leaving you here. You don't have to earn love anymore." The girl behind the glass didn't need to be rescued. She needed to be kept.

And on that floor, mascara streaking down my face, lungs gasping for air, I said " I am sorry I abandoned you. I am sorry I didn't protect you. I am sorry I betrayed you. I am here now, I am here to stay" I was filled with a peace that surpasses all understanding. It came like a presence that had already been there, I knew it was HIM. The panic loosened its grip. My breathing slowed without effort. The room felt held. The ache was still there, but it no longer demanded to be fixed. It softened. It rested. I felt known in a way that didn't require words. Seen without being examined. Loved without performing. I was being gathered, not corrected. The words I had rehearsed for years, "you have to try harder, you have to earn this, don't be too much" were nowhere to be found. In their place was something gentle. True. Unshaken by the mess on the floor. The part of me that had been bracing finally rested, as if I had been placed in arms stronger than my own, arms that didn't grow tired of my tears. I understood then, not with logic, but with certainty, I was not alone in my breaking. I was chosen, picked up from the floor, pursued by goodness and mercy, held tightly in security.

A Love Letter That Rebuilt Me

I didn't leave that night transformed. I drifted into sleep feeling safe to feel. Aware that something holy had begun, but not finished. Healing didn't arrive as a single revelation, but as an invitation to come near.

In the days that followed, I noticed how often my thoughts turned against me. How quickly old beliefs tried to reclaim their place. I would wake up steady, then unravel by noon. Certain one moment, doubting the next. But each time the noise rose, there was a gentle interruption. It was as if God was reaching for me with phrases that stayed with me long after prayer had ended. In quiet assurance that didn't erase the pain, but reframed it. I began to write them down. They were the love letters my heart was yearning for. God spoke my love language generously.

Love Letter One — You Are Not Held Together by Others

My Precious Beloved,

I see how often you scan the room before you breathe.

How quickly you adjust yourself to keep peace.

How your heart learned to measure safety by who stays.

But I want you to know this:

You are not sustained by human closeness. You are sustained by Me.

I do not withdraw when you feel weak.

I do not leave when your emotions rise.

I do not require your constant effort to remain near.

Let Me carry what you were never meant to manage alone.

You do not need to cling to be kept.

I am not going anywhere.

Now Rest.

With Endearing Love,

Your Heavenly Father

Fear not, for I am with you; be not dismayed, for I am your God. I will strengthen you, I will help you, I will uphold you with My righteous right hand.—Isaiah 41:10

Joy Comes in the Morning

The sun was just breaking over the buildings in downtown Elgin. The streets were quiet. My breath was steady, air was crisp, feet hitting pavement rhythmically. I was replaying old conversations in my mind—things I should have said, things I wish I could've done. And then, it hit me mid-stride: You cannot out-love someone's free will. God Himself does not force transformation. He draws. He convicts. He corrects. WHY did I think I could? Why am I in the same situation AGAIN? I slowed down, hands on my hips, heart pounding. That is when it was revealed to me. It wasn't up to me to decide the outcomes for life. I needed to focus on obedience.

The first time I ran a 5K, it took me 47 minutes. My lungs burned. My legs felt heavy. My thoughts were louder than my footsteps, and when I finished, I collapsed on the grass.

So week after week, I walked, I jogged, I sprinted. I cried, I laughed, I radiated. Somewhere between mile one and mile three, the narrative began to change. "You're getting stronger." "You can do hard things."

Twelve minutes disappeared from my time over the next few months. Thirty-five minutes and thirty seconds. That clock didn't just measure speed. It measured healing. God wasn't just strengthening my legs. He was rebuilding my discipline. My identity. My resilience. What started as therapy in motion turned into community. One morning after a run through downtown Elgin, I looked around at the women stretching beside me. Mothers, entrepreneurs. I thought, "Don't keep this to yourself." So, I started a running club. There is a version of me that could have stayed comfortable. Part-time effort. Part-time belief. Part-time dreams, but comfort started to feel like a cage. At 5:00 a.m. my anxiety would wake me. I felt like I had to sit myself up quickly, hold my chest tightly, and take deep breaths. I know God did not design me to wake up like this. I began to turn my mornings over to him. For devotion and prayer. Day by day, peace slowly returned. I learned that joy truly comes in the morning.

When Rejection Became Sacred

There was a time when rejection felt like a personal indictment. If someone walked away, betrayed my trust, or chose distance instead of commitment, my instinct was to internalize it. It felt like being pushed outside of something I desperately wanted to belong to. But as my faith deepened, something unexpected began to happen. My perspective started to change.

One morning, while reading the Gospels, I noticed something I had read many times before but never truly felt. The very people He came to love doubted Him. Religious leaders mocked Him. Crowds praised Him one day and abandoned Him the next. One of His closest companions betrayed Him for silver. And suddenly, the pain I had been carrying began to look different. When I felt rejected, I began to remember that

Jesus was rejected first.

When I felt betrayed, I remembered that someone who walked beside Him daily still turned against Him. When I felt pushed aside or misunderstood, I remembered that the Son of God Himself experienced far more. What once felt humiliating began to feel strangely sacred. It was in that moment when I was on the floor with mascara streaming down my face that I felt closest to Jesus. Not because suffering is something we should chase, but because it reminded me that I was not alone inside it. The Savior I pray to is not distant from human pain. He stepped into it. He carried it. He understands it from the inside. He knows what it feels like to love deeply and still be misunderstood. He knows what it feels like to give and not be received. He knows what it feels like to be faithful when others walk away. And somehow that realization transformed my wounds into something different.

Instead of asking, why did this happen to me? I began asking, what is God shaping in me through this? Instead of feeling discarded, I began to feel refined. Every moment of rejection pushed me closer to the only love that has never abandoned me. The love of Christ does not disappear when people do. When I began to see rejection through that lens, something unexpected happened, the pain lost its power to define me. It became a doorway instead. A doorway into deeper faith. Deeper humility. Deeper intimacy with the One who truly understands.

If I close my eyes, I can still feel the woman at the beginning of this story. Collapsed on the ground with tears falling faster than she could wipe them away. Her chest tight, her heart aching, wondering how something that once felt so full of promise could leave her feeling so empty.

What felt like despair was actually the beginning of God's gentle rescue. Every tear that fell that night watered the soil of a life He was about to grow. The heartbreak that once felt like the end of my story was quietly becoming the place where healing would begin.

God does not remove something from our lives just to leave us with emptiness. He removes what does not align so He can make space for something far greater. Today, I no longer cling to what is leaving. I release it with open hands and a trusting heart. The same heart that once broke in sorrow now beats with hope. Where there was once confusion, there is clarity. Where there was once longing, there is peace. Where there was once grief, there is growth.

I see now that God was never taking love away from me. He was leading me toward the kind of love that heals, restores, and never abandons. The woman who once cried herself to sleep now walks forward differently, not afraid of what she might lose, but excited for what God is preparing.

The most beautiful chapters of our lives begin in the raw moments where we finally release what we thought we needed and trust that God is writing something even more beautiful than we could ever imagine.

Reflection

What do you see when you look in the mirror?

If you had to write a letter to yourself, what would you say?

What are the things you are holding on to that are not aligned with your destiny?

About the Author

Vanessa Martinez-Torres, is a first-generation Latina college graduate in STEM, she is a real estate agent and investor based in Elgin, Illinois, driven by faith, resilience, and purpose. As a mother, she is committed to building a life rooted in growth while inspiring others to do the same.

Her writing blends emotional honesty with spiritual reflection, exploring identity, healing, and purpose. Through her work, she creates a space where vulnerability meets strength, encouraging women, especially those navigating self-worth and personal growth, to embrace their depth and recognize their value.

Her mission is to remind others of their worth, inspire confidence, and encourage a life led with faith and intention.

CHAPTER 5

It's All About the Turkey

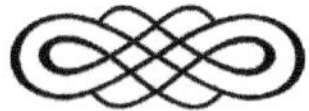

Uni Camacho

"When you live in darkness, you separate yourself from those who live in the light."

Scripture says life is like a vapor, It's there and it's gone. I didn't understand what it meant, but life was on a voyage to explain that to me. On October 9, 1997, I got a phone call. My life came to a halt. "Your husband was in a motorcycle accident", they said. "What" I said? At that moment I was thinking my husband doesn't like motorcycles, he didn't own one. I was shocked and dismayed. But of course, it did happen. Carlos was visiting his father in Chicago. The neighbor owned a motorcycle. He coerced him to take a ride around the block. To my understanding, the neighbor pleaded with him because he initially didn't want to go. Carlos did go and never came back. As they were at the stop, with his blinkers turning left and waiting for the traffic to pass to return to the street his father lived on, a drunk driver in a van running from the cops hit the motorcycle. It was a head on collision. The neighbor died instantly. Four days later, Carlos died from the complications of it. You know...one of the biggest fears in my life was to be a single parent. My number one prayer as a child was that I didn't want to be a single parent. The reality came to pass. I am now a single parent. God has a sense of humor.

I had a promising future. I wanted to finish college. The goal was to be a physical therapist and open an outpatient facility. That was now a pipe dream. Tragedy struck. Now, I am a widow at the age of twenty-six years old, my children being five, six and nine years old, my oldest being a special needs child. Now I am facing the very cry that I feared the most...a single-family home. I was devastated.

I lost all sense of hope. At this point in your life, your job is to survive, not to thrive. But how? How am I going to navigate this? John 15:5 says, “I am the vine, you are the branches. He who abides in Me, and I in him, bears much fruit; for without Me, you can do nothing”. I was a Christ follower. I loved God. I can honestly say, I didn’t question God on why it happened. I accepted it. What I didn’t know was that this experience would take me on a dark path. A path I don’t wish on even my worst enemies. I lost all sense of reality. I started to drink. I started to do drugs. I started to hang out with people who were not on the mission to succeed in life. I was lost for five years of my life. When you cross over to the dark side, you become blinded by what's real. It’s almost like a film, covering your eyes. You don’t see life the same. And when you’re in this darkness, you become so broken and so strayed that you vanquish the very person of who you were. I disappeared and I was nowhere to be found.

God bless my family. They were praying for me fervently, my mother and siblings. When death comes knocking on your door. If someone has not experienced this, there’s nothing one can say to make things better. Unless you experience it yourself. At least, that's how I felt. I love them very much! James 5:16 says, “The effectual fervent prayer of a righteous man availeth much”.

It got so bad that I created phobias in my life. I was scared to drive. Driving in the rain and snow was so frightening, that I would go into a state of uncontrollable panic. It was debilitating. I didn't want to be around people. Didn't trust everything and anything. I remember feeling so destitute that I didn't see the light of day. And in that darkness...all you feel is hopelessness, shame and guilt. All you want to do is come back to the light, but you don't know how to get there.

I had decided. I was going to take my life. I wasn't worthy of life. My two children were living with my sister at the time. My intention was to do it on Christmas. How selfish is that. At least, that was my intent. One evening, a close friend of mine who lived in Missouri by the name of Brenda McClain was woken up by the Holy Spirit. The Holy Spirit is God's voice. He told her to write me a letter. She was obedient to the request. You see...she didn't know what was going on in my life. When you live in darkness, you separate yourself from those who live in the light.

As the day was approaching, I was making my plans. A letter came in the mail. It was the day before Christmas. When I opened the letter, it was like a spotlight from the heavens. I was in awe of the words I was reading. The letter stated that I had the love of God in me and through me. My worship to the Father was beautiful. The joy that I have. The love of life that I lived. I kept reading. God spoke through those words like it was coming forth like a rushing wind. At that moment, God reminded me of who I was, not what I was.

God loves me not for what I am, but who I am! Instantaneously, my heart was healed! My guilt, shame and hopelessness was gone. I knew that I knew great things are coming! Joel 2:25 says, "God will restore all the wasted years that the locust has eaten up". God had turned my heart of stone to a heart of flesh and gave me a new spirit, Ezekiel 36:26. Instructions of healing and restorations came. I became a new person in Christ Jesus! Hallelujah!!

Past Experiences, Leads to Gifts, Leads to Good Works

When a transformation happens in your heart, it doesn't change the manifestations you created. You look around your world and it's still dark, but now with your newfound HOPE; you don't see darkness the same way. You see a way out. You give yourself an abundance of grace. Jeremiah 33:3 says, "Call to me, I will answer you, and show you great and mighty things, which you don't know". I lived like a vampire, I slept during the day, and I was up at night. So, the next day, even though I had been up all night...I saw daylight! The light was so good! What joy to see light! I had accomplished my first goal! It was so euphoric! One by one small tangible goals at a time, I gave to myself. Day by day I began to grow like a tree planted by the river. My roots started to thicken. The primary root started to lengthen, and the secondary root was widening. My foundation was set. I was ready to go get my children. And I did!

It took me one year to go into the house of God since I found my new Hope. I started attending support and recovery classes. It was years of learning personal behavior. The books I went through had psychology principles with a biblical base worldview. My tree had begun to grow branches full of luscious leaves. I started to understand my purpose in life. See...our experiences in life become stepping stools to our future. We take those experiences by forgiving ourselves, forgiving others with empathy and it becomes a driving force. My experiences evolved to a gift. I morphed to gratefulness. I became grateful for the opportunities that God allowed me to experience. I understood why for the first time, even though I never asked why. You love differently. A profound sense of peace that passes all understanding. My motto in life is...past experiences, leads to gifts, leads to good works. I now am a light in a dark world to help people come to the light. Romans 8:28 says, "And we know that all things work together for the good to those who love God, to those who are called according to His purpose". I live a purpose driven life. God is so good! And I am in awe of the Greatness of God!!

My Kingdom Assignment

Psalms 90:17 says, "May the favor of the Lord our God rest on us; establish the work of our hands, yes, establish the work of our hands". I started serving where there was a need in the church. All I wanted to do is to give back. Greeting was my first volunteer job. My special needs son, Isaac was my sidekick. His smile is radiant! I loved greeting people when they walked in the house of God. I was so grateful to do it. My heart melted with prevailing love. I couldn't help myself. It was coming out of my pours. I felt in my spirit, I wanted to do more.

One early morning, our pastor gave a challenge. A kingdom assignment. This was a 6 multi-location church. He asked for 100 volunteers, given $100 each, what would you do for the kingdom. Of course, I stood up like a rocket. I knew right away what the Holy Spirit instilled in me. My kingdom assignment was to help single families. I had an opportunity to make a difference in four families. I sent out an email and shared that they couldn't afford Christmas. They needed necessities like coats, hats, gloves, etc. The response was enormous. Sponsors came out of the woodwork! The total amount of money collected and spent was $750. On Christmas day, my children and I spent our day going from house to house delivering these wonderful gifts to these great people. It was intimidating to say the least. We stood there watching them open the presents as tears ran from the mothers' faces. I told everyone of the mothers' that God chose them and loves them. It was amazing. And that was the beginning! I was compelled to do more.

Before we go any further, let's zoom out for a moment. Let's take a step back and look at the full picture. As a child, life was challenging. Learning how to adjust in a one parent household after my parents got divorced was hardening. Even worse, living in an environment where you were ridiculed, bullied and not accepted because of the color of my skin. In elementary school, there was a gym teacher by the name of Linda Gates. She saw the emptiness in my life and decided to become my mentor. She went out of her way and gave me positive affirmations when I needed it the most. She pushed me to be better. One of my most memorable words that still generates in my spirit today is, "to get out of your own way." I didn't understand it then as I do today. When vitality came back to my heart after the death of my husband, the Holy Spirit reminded me everything that woman told me as a child came to life. Now, let's start painting the bigger picture. After my experience with helping the four families we impacted and my encounter with Linda, I was determined to find Christian mentors for Isaac, Monique and Alex, my beloved children.

As I researched, I realized there was not a mentoring program in the local area. I went to my pastor and asked if I could start one. He agreed. I found two national organizations that help and support churches establish mentoring programs. Their purpose is to link at-risk children from single parent homes with Christian mentors. So, in September 2005, we launched 10:17 Youth Mentoring. We served hundreds of children, including my own. What a glorious site to see! There's a superpower one receives when you have a mentor outside the home. In 2007, we were nominated as one of the best mentoring programs in the country. For the next twenty years, I worked with local, regional and national mentoring programs. Psalms 82:3 says, A call to defend the weak and the fatherless; uphold the cause of the poor and the oppressed". I was commissioned to protect and to defend. And as this chapter closed,

I was left with deep gratitude knowing it was an honor to contribute to something bigger than myself. God be the Glory!!

The Turkey

While I am grateful for the past, I'm equally excited about what comes next. See...till this point, I never owned a home. Mi Casa. I was so busy working for the Father, that it never crossed my mind that it was equally significant. In those days, my mother was sick and needed help. She had convinced me to get out of my apartment and move in with her. With much prayer, I said yes. I set the date, got my stuff in storage and we were off. I remember walking up to the door and knocking. She opened the door, looked at me and said, "I changed my mind", and closed the door. I stared at the door in utter disbelief. For the first time in my life, I am homeless. Psalms 86:7 says, "In the day of trouble, I will call upon thee: for thou wilt answer me". I cried out to the Lord like a baby crying for their momma. In these moments, my friends, when someone pulls the rug right under you and you fall, what do you do? Well...you get up and continue to live. I was very active in those days. Director of a mentoring program, serving in the church, had my own business, working at a boxing club and completing my duties as Mrs. Puerto Rico 2010-2011 (that is for another story time:)).

It was Thanksgiving. I agreed to bake a turkey for a community dinner. I was staying in a basement. As I was making this turkey, tears were running down my cheeks like a broken facet. I pulled up to the church. I didn't want to see anyone. It was too hard to hold my emotions within. There was a man by the name Rick Guzman who took the turkey from me. It felt like he saw right through me. He handed the turkey to someone, and unbeknownst to me, he hugged me. I burst into tears and cried out, "I'm homeless and I don't know what to do, I'm homeless"!! With his kind and caring words, he said, "It's going to be alright...It's going to be alright". What I didn't know, this was a divine moment from God. A supernatural breath of God. That man is an Executive Director for a nonprofit organization that paves the way for first time home buyers. That same week, I was in my own place. I joined his program and in 2015, I bought my first home. Jeremiah 29:11 says, "I will give you hope and future."

My impact on the Aurora, Illinois community and beyond, has been the embodiment of my motto. Partnering with local churches to help "adopt the block" missions to fill practical needs. I recently joined teams in Iquitos, Peru working in communities along the Amazon to provide access to clean water by digging wells. Now, within the next phase of life I am continuing to do disaster relief work with the focus in communities in the US. I am currently serving as a board member to the very organization that helped me get out of homelessness.

Above all, my heart goes back to my family and their future. I am married now to a God-fearing man of fourteen years, my love Alejandro. A dedicated mother and grandmother of four,

Positioning in stability and building generational wealth by becoming a real estate investor.

I will leave you with this...there is life after death. God brings dead bones back to life. And life more abundantly. Your experiences are gifts. Use them, and God will put the last missing pieces of your puzzle in life back together.

For the Kingdom.

Reflection

What do you think is the essence of life?

What changes do you hope to make to make your life better and worthwhile?

What is your kingdom assignment?

About the Author

Uni Camacho is a faith-driven writer, mentor, and community leader from Aurora, Illinois. Once homeless, she overcame adversity to become a homeowner, national powerlifting champion, and President of a nonprofit boxing organization that empowers youth through discipline and faith.

A missionary, Deaconess, and lifelong mentor, she writes powerful stories of redemption rooted in truth, transformation, and hope. Her mission is to show that your past does not disqualify you, it can become your testimony.

CHAPTER 6

Finding Myself at the Finish Line

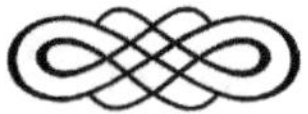

Cynthia Hernandez

"I took a deep breath and knew I was going to finish that race one way or another."

Life happened and here I am almost 50 years old. Mother of three beautiful, smart and determined children, a 4-time Chicago marathon finisher to which only 0.01% of the global population has completed. I finally found who I am and what fills my heart with joy. Knowing what my purpose is took time but it arrived.

My son Michael got home from school with homework about Katherine Switzer, the first woman to officially run the Boston marathon in 1967. He asked me what a marathon was and I told him it was a race where you complete 26.2 miles. Michael looked up at me with curls in his forehead and with a very firm voice said "Mommy you can run a marathon" I replied without hesitation "Of course mi amor. Mommy can run a marathon". I had no clue how I was going to do it but I knew that the day would come when I would tell my son, "see Mommy ran a marathon." The idea to run a marathon started that day.

I was invited to a networking event but wasn't sure I wanted to go. Many of the attendees were real estate agents, brokers, business owners, people with a career and a college education. Everything that I wasn't and didn't have. I was just a stay at home mom, soccer mom, PTA mom with no college degree or career.

As I arrived the anxiety started to get the best of me. I was beautifully dressed for the occasion but what could I contribute or have in common with everyone in that room. What would I talk about, soccer, my teenagers and toddler? I wasn't sure I wanted to be there. I had nothing to contribute to conversations and thought about turning back and going home. Jennifer called me to where she was with a group of people. I felt nervous walking towards them. With a big smile she said "This is Cynthia SHE IS A RUNNER! Everyone in shock looked at me to wait and see what I would say. My eyes opened up, time stood still for a moment and my heartbeat went a little faster. I quickly started talking about training, runs by the lake, all the running communities and the support I received from them. I knew who I was when I heard it out loud. A RUNNER! At the end of the evening as I drove home I couldn't help but smile. For the first time in a long time I knew who Cynthia was and what I wanted to continue doing.

Thanks to my sister Erica I started my running journey and have been doing it for 14 years. I ran my first race with my sisters in March of 2012.

We didn't train very much but we got to the finish line. The feeling of crossing the finish line that day changed something inside me. The adrenaline was so high and I wanted to feel that again. It felt great and it was me doing all the work a step at a time. The following years I ran a few more races, most of them were with my three sisters, sometimes two, sometimes one and all of a sudden it was only myself running them. My daughter Michelle and I started running a 5k in Pilsen for about three years. I loved that mommy/daughter bonding time with her. Seeing her pass me up and cross the finish line first at only 8 years old filled my heart with joy. The day came in 2022 when I would run my first Chicago marathon. I told myself to just run and finish those 26.2 miles. Bought new shoes a week before which ended up being too tight. It was a very lonely race. I was going through a divorce and had so many thoughts in my mind. All I knew was that I would cross that finish line and prove to myself I could do it. My heart was shattered into a million pieces but something about running and hearing the crowds cheer for me without knowing me made the pieces start going into place. What I thought was a small rock in my shoe during the race ended up being a huge bloody blister. I skipped, hopped and dragged my feet to the finish line. I didn't know anyone at the time. I thank my sister Carime who went to pick me and took me home. I completed my second marathon in 2023 suffering from plantar fasciitis. The pain was unbearable, I thought about stopping half way through so many times. Quitting wasn't a choice for me. I knew I would finish it one way or another and I did. I enjoyed training in 2024 with different running clubs and new friends. Got to feel confetti from a popper for the first time during a half marathon thanks to Jon. I was so ready for the marathon that year. I saw my family cheer from the crowds for the first time. I hit a PR. I was so proud of that achievement. Training in 2025 didn't go as planned and a few injuries held me back. I ended up with a stomach flu two days before the marathon. Maybe I should have stayed home that morning but I don't quit very easily. I knew I had to get to the

Mexican consulate close to mile 15 because my family was there again. That pushed me mile after mile. I saw my mom raising and waiving the Mexican flag so proudly waiting for her daughter and my sisters and nieces with beautiful posters. I ran to her and hugged her like a little girl and told her crying in tears "Mom ya no puedo estoy bien cansada." I was tired and wanted to stop, my stomach hurt so much I couldn't bear the pain any longer. She hugged me in a way she hadn't hugged me in such a long time and said "Mija tu si puedes hechale ganas!" I took a deep breath and knew I was going to finish that race one way or another. I waited for my kids for about 30 minutes since they lost me in the crowds trying to cheer for me a few miles back. I had to hug them tight and thank them for running and biking two miles to see their mother run a marathon. The unconditional support the running community gave me was incredible. My friend Fed, who also was running the marathon, stepped off the course to buy me something to drink because he saw how much I was struggling. My cheerful friend Silvia who gave me a torta and ran and walked two miles with me made me forget the pain I was feeling all over my body. Claudia and Dahlia waited for hours with a coke and gave me a warm hug. Everyone in the running community cheered me on like I was going to finish first place. Finally Sergio and Erika who waited for me to finish hours after they had finished themselves. I told them to leave but Sergio texted me "We came together we leave together" they waited and we went to eat. Those friendships are priceless and will stay in my heart forever. One day I went to present my medals to my grandmother and explained what a marathon was. She held my hands tightly and said "mi nieta la mas ganadora." My granddaughter is the winner. Those words will always be with me at every race. Rest in peace Abuelita Antonia you were loved and will always be remembered by so many.

45 AND PREGNANT! I was going to have a baby when many of my friends were becoming grandmothers. I received looks that almost said you are too old. I felt they were right and the embarrassment started to add up. I was ashamed and embarrassed in silence. I kept it out of social media during all my pregnancy. Do I regret it? Of course! I don't have many pictures of my belly. I didn't want the world to know yet. I just wasn't ready for all the questions. I was scared something would go wrong again. Years back I had a miscarriage with twins and it impacted my life so much. I didn't know how to cope or mourn. All I could do was put my emotions on mute and block everything so it wouldn't hurt. I knew the day would come when I couldn't hold on to my emotions inside and I would let them out unexpectedly. I cried until my eyes felt dry that night and I was finally able to grieve my loss. I was so scared that it would happen again. Now I was much older and the risk was much higher. I tried to embrace my pregnancy but I had so many complications along the way that I just couldn't handle it. I had a high risk pregnancy, gestational diabetes, and high blood pressure. It was too much to handle and I didn't know how to ask for help. My emotions got the best of me for so many days. What was wrong with me? I should be happy and embrace my pregnancy like I did with my two other children. Marko arrived and I knew why I

needed him so much in my life. He is the one who gives me random hugs and kisses and tells me I love mommy when I need it the most.

Everything happens for a reason, something my mom has always said to me. Things did happen and it felt like I received a direct red card from life that I knew. That's how I felt being married for 16 years and having to accept it was coming to an end. Now years later I accept it was best for both of us. It was extremely hard for me to accept it in the beginning. I was on my own with two preteens and a baby. I had to take responsibility for my home and had to step up one way or another. What would happen to our families during the holidays and their birthdays? So many questions and I had no answers at the time. Now of course I see everything in a different perspective. I am raising my children to the best of my knowledge. Not entirely alone because they will always have mom and dad who support them unconditionally. They are blessed to have supportive grandparents that love having them over, especially Marko. Grandma calls to have him over to spend time with them all the time. Those are beautiful memories for him to have. All of this has made me live a different life and step out of my comfort zone to become the best version of myself. I am grateful for the chapters that I lived while married. We were blessed with three amazing children and memories that will last a lifetime. And now it's time to make more memories in my new chapters.

How was I able to have a baby at the age of 45, process a divorce, raise a family and run a marathon four times? One word: God. Each time I said my prayers I asked for guidance and to have my path enlightened. I know He is always by my side and my faith will always be stronger than ever. I have so much to be thankful for. Thank you to Michelle and Michael for helping so much with Marko. You three are my world and I promise I will always be there for you. My family for all their unconditional support. My Mother Elena for being a great example of what a strong hardworking woman and mother is. I thank my running community for always cheering me on. I will always be thankful that our paths were crossed. But I'm not done yet...

Reflection

In a room full of people, who are you?

What achievements do you downplay?

Are you proud of who you are?

About the Author

Cynthia Hernandez is an author, educator, and passionate runner who has completed over 70 races, including multiple half-marathons and four Chicago Marathons.

Born in Guerrero, Mexico, and raised in Chicago, she writes to inspire others through stories of faith, resilience, and personal growth. A devoted mother of three, she is committed to encouraging others, especially first-time runners to believe in themselves and pursue their goals with courage and purpose.

CHAPTER 7

I Refused to Stay Down:

A True Story of Faith, Survival, and Rising Against the Odds

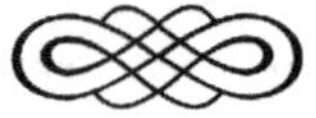

Isaly Marie Juanche

"The faith I carry is quiet and consistent.
It is rooted in reverence for God"

I am a woman, a mother of three children—two daughters and one son. I am a wife, a daughter, and a sister. I am also an entrepreneur in real estate. I am 32 years old, and the strength people often see in me was not something I was born with. It was built through pain, endurance, and faith.

This is a short recap of my life that I will be diving into deeper later. But to understand me, you need to know what shaped me. I have come to believe that God chooses His strongest warriors not because they are fearless, but because they are willing to trust Him even when the battle feels unbearable. God gives His best warriors His hardest battles, not to break them, but to shape them.

Looking back now, I can see that God has been forming me since the day I was born. At the time, I didn't understand it. As a child, I only knew that life felt heavy earlier than it should. Today, as a woman and a mother, I understand that God was never absent—He was preparing me.

I remember the day I was baptized clearly. I was not a baby; I was already around eleven years old. There is a photograph from that day that my family has kept. In it, something appears on my forehead—something that stood out enough that the pastor who baptized me spoke to my father afterward. He told him that I had been chosen by God.

At the time, those words meant nothing to me. I was just a child. Today, I understand that being chosen does not mean being spared from pain. It means being trusted with purpose.

The Diagnosis

The first time my faith was truly shaken was the day they called and asked me to come into my gynecologist's office.

They wouldn't say why. I already knew something was not right because doctors do not ask you to come in for good news.

When they finally walked in, their faces said it before their mouths did.

"All I heard was the word cancer."

One word. One sentence.

And my entire world split in two. They told me everything would be okay, just like that. But it's not the same as telling me not to research it. Well, I should have listened because that made things worse for me.

My daughter was only a year and a half old. She still needed me for everything. She still reached for me in the middle of the night. She still called for me when she was scared.

And all I could think was: What if I don't get to watch her grow up? I'm going to die at stage 4! And the doctor said it like it was normal. Nothing!

I went home and tried to act normal. I made dinner. I bathed my baby. I held her longer than usual. When she fell asleep, I went into the bathroom, locked the door, and cried so hard I couldn't breathe.

At night, the fear was louder. I didn't want no one to hear me. I thought I was overthinking it because that's what my husband told me. He said the doctor said you were going to be fine.

So, I had to cry and pray alone.

I prayed through tears.

I begged God to let me stay.

Not for me — for my child.

I had plans and dreams, including bringing my father to the United States so he could be with me. In a moment, everything I envisioned for my future felt uncertain.

I remember thinking, this cannot be happening—not now. Not when my life was just beginning. Not when my daughter needed me. Not when my family still depended on me. My husband is the type that does not like to tell nobody nothing. So obviously I went through this in silence. I didn't even tell my father. No one!

Now that I'm writing this, people might think I'm crazy for keeping something like that inside. I'm not even sure that was the best decision. Looking back, I don't know if that was healthy. Keeping something that big inside caused pain I didn't deal with. I was trying to be strong. Trying to be the woman who holds everything together.

By the grace of God, I was able to have surgery and have it removed. I don't fully understand how everything aligned the way it did — the timing, the doctors, the strength I didn't know I had. I'm blessed, I said.

Today, I know with certainty that God knew it was not my time. There was still life for me to live. More love to give. More purpose to fulfill. That changed me forever. It taught me that faith is not the absence of fear, but the decision to trust God even while fear is present.

As life continued, the challenges did not disappear. I became a mother again. I built a family. I carried responsibilities, sacrifices, and worries that no one else could see. I learned that strength does not always look loud or confident. Sometimes strength looks like continuing to show up—tired, uncertain, but faithful.

My faith today is not perfect, and it is not performed. It is not built on appearances or words meant to impress others. I have seen faith spoken without love and belief practiced without compassion. That is not the faith I live by.

The faith I carry is quiet and consistent. It is rooted in reverence for God, in responsibility, in integrity, and in love for others. I believe in God, and I believe in the saints who remind me that holiness is formed through suffering, perseverance, and grace. I believe that God has never abandoned me, even when life tested me beyond what I thought I could endure.

Recovery Room

During my second pregnancy, after my baby was born and they took me to the recovery room, I had a severe hemorrhage. Several doctors rushed in at once. Everything started moving very quickly. They took the baby from my husband's hands, and he stood in the corner while I was bleeding.

I remember the doctor asking me how I felt. I remember the nurses moving fast. I heard someone say, "Add fluids on her," and they increased the IV fluids.

There was a lot of blood loss. They had to numb me and manually remove the blood clots to help stop the bleeding. It was uncomfortable and overwhelming, but I understood they were trying to stabilize me. After that, I told my father, "Dad, you almost lost your princess."

He said, "What do you mean?" And I told him everything.

He said to me over the phone, "Oh my... I prayed for you, baby. Nothing would ever happen to you. And before God thinks of taking you, I will ask for an exchange for my life."

My Father

My dream was to bring my father to the United States. He had but one leg. When I left him, I promised him I would do everything to bring him with me. God is my witness that I tried my best. I worked so hard to qualify so I could petition for him.

One week after I gave birth to my second daughter, I got the worst phone call. The one phone call I never wanted to get.

And I got it.

My father had passed away before I could bring him. I lost myself at that moment. But I could not stay lost. I had a four-year-old daughter and a newborn baby girl waiting for me at home. I had a husband. I had a business that needed this whole woman, even when she was broken.

Imagine needing to be there for everyone when I could not even hold myself together. I had to fly to Mexico with my siblings to cremate him. That was the worst and longest flight I have ever taken. Everything felt against us at that moment. Imagine waiting two hours on the plane before it departed, just because one of my brothers was in Alaska, in a different time zone, while we were here in Chicago — all so we could arrive in Mexico City at the same time.

Call it crazy, but we knew it was my father wanting us all to arrive together, not separately. Because if the plane would have departed on time we would have arrived first before my brother and not all 4 of his children at the same time.

Trust me when they say you can't feel what it feels like losing a parent until you lose a parent. Losing our father was like we lost our world because he was our mother and father, that man raised four children on his own. No Manual, nothing. Just him and God on his side! I write these lines in his honor. I want the world to know he was the best father we could ever ask for. And his baby girl will make him proud.

When 2024 Brought Me to My Knees

The year 2024 came, and life really shook me. It made me fall to my knees and beg God to save my third child — my baby boy, my last child. He was just two months old.

Since he was born, he had been constantly throwing up milk. My mother's instinct kept telling me something was wrong. I was constantly taking him to the pediatrician, watching, worrying, listening to that quiet voice inside me: Your baby needs help.

One day I told my husband, "Let's take the baby to the hospital. I don't think he looks good." I got a family member to stay with our two girls, and we headed to the hospital. While we were driving, my baby stopped responding. My husband realized we weren't going to make it in time and said, "You have to give him CPR."

I had never done CPR before in my life. And now I needed to save my son. I started CPR. I was losing him. I told my husband he's not responding, what do I do? He said keep doing it. My soul felt like it was dying. By God's grace...I brought him back.

My husband flagged down a police officer and stopped in front of the car. I jumped out holding my baby, handing him over to the police for help.

It's like God was there. The ambulance was like 2 min away.

We got into the ambulance, and my husband followed us to the first hospital. In the emergency room, the only way he wouldn't lose consciousness was if he stayed on top of me. Even during the CT scans, he remained on my chest while the doctors worked around us.

Then the emergency doctor came in. He told us there was blood in my baby's brain. I couldn't even process it.

How?

Why?

They told us he needed emergency surgery and had to be transferred to another hospital that specialized in babies. They did everything with him still on top of me. I rode in the ambulance alone with him. My husband had to drive separately.

Walking through those emergency doors felt like a nightmare. Going through those doors as they opened one by one and me on the side walking with my baby holding his little hand.

When we arrived, the neurosurgeon met us. I held his hand and said, "May God guide this operation." He told me, "I will do the best I can... but say goodbye to him." I remember telling my baby, "You can't leave me, Mommy will be waiting for you," and I kissed his forehead. That goodbye was not going to be the end — not while I still had hope.

In the waiting room, my husband and I just held each other. I got on my knees and begged God. I prayed to my father: Since you are with God, you have to intervene for us. You cannot allow this to happen, save your grandson!!

Those were the longest hours of my life. My soul was tired. After long hours of wait. Then the doctor walked in. "The operation was a success."

Relief washed over me, but it wasn't over.

Here in the United States, when something like this happens, parents are questioned first. In the middle of my worst nightmare, I had to fight again. But I stood strong. Now we had to fight the DCFS process. Because when you survive the moments where you almost lose your life, and the moments where you almost lose your child, you are never the same woman again. Story to be continued. Thank you for reading my story.

Reflection

What do you think are the struggles of being a woman, a wife, or a mother?

How can we make life much more bearable for ourselves?

What are you doing to build and maintain the relationships in your life?

About the Author

Isaly Marie Juanche is a general contractor, real estate investor, and self-general contractor coach passionate about empowering women to confidently lead their own construction and real estate projects. With hands-on experience in residential development, she brings practical knowledge and real-world insight to her work.

She is a co-author of Latinas in Construction and a contributor to Wise Women Empower Women, where she shares faith-driven insights on growth, leadership, and purpose. As a wife and mother of three—two daughters and one son—her life is rooted in faith, family, and resilience. Her children are her greatest joy and motivation, and her husband—her "partner in crime"—is her safe place, truth, and greatest support.

She is also the daughter of a man who is no longer physically by her side but lives through everything she does. In honor of her father, Alberto, she continues to move with purpose, carrying his memory in her heart.

Through her writing and work, she inspires women to trust God, embrace growth, and step into their purpose with confidence and intention.

CHAPTER 8

Cracked But Called

From Survival to Surrender: A Journey of Healing Through God's Love

Maria Elena Ramirez

"Survival is not the same as living."

Dedication

This chapter is dedicated to every woman and man who has ever felt abandoned, unseen, unloved, or broken by life's circumstances. To those who grew up too fast. To those who learned to survive before they learned how to live. To those who built emotional walls just to feel safe. May this testimony remind you that no matter how deep the cracks in your heart may be, God is able to heal, restore, and make all things new.

Introduction

There are wounds we carry that no one can see.

Wounds from broken promises.

Wounds from abandonment.

Wounds from growing up too fast.

Wounds from being told—directly or indirectly—that we are not wanted, not protected, not loved.

For many years, I lived my life in survival mode. I didn't know what it meant to feel safe emotionally. I didn't know how to trust others. And I certainly didn't know how to trust God. My heart had become a collection of invisible cracks formed by childhood trauma, rejection, fear, poverty, and loneliness.

On the outside, I was functioning. I was working. I was showing up for life.

But on the inside, I was fractured.

I grew up believing that love was temporary, that people always leave, and that depending on anyone was dangerous. So I made a vow to myself at a very young age: I will survive on my own. That vow protected me—but it also imprisoned me.

Because survival is not the same as living.

This book is not about pretending pain never happened.

This book is about what happens when pain meets the presence of God.

It is about forgiveness that feels impossible.

Healing that takes time.

Faith that grows slowly in the middle of doubt.

And a love that does not abandon you—even when others do.

I share my story not because I have it all together, but because I know what it feels like to be broken—and to be held together by God's grace. My prayer is that as you read these pages, you will see yourself not through the lens of your past, but through the truth of God's love.

Whether you are a believer, questioning your faith, or unsure if God even sees you, I want you to know this:

You are not too damaged to be healed.

You are not too far gone to be restored.

And you are not alone.

God specializes in mending cracked hearts.

Cracked but Called: From Survival to Healing

Growing up, life was not easy.

I was raised in a single-parent home, and from a very young age, I learned what it meant to survive. Survival mode wasn't something I stepped into later in life—it was the only life I knew. We didn't have much. My mother worked long hours at a factory during the day, and at night she ironed clothes for extra money just to keep a roof over our heads and food on the table. Yet somehow, she always found a way to celebrate my birthday each year—even if it was just with a homemade cake and juice. Those small moments became sacred memories. They were reminders that even in lack, there could still be love.

But my childhood forced me to grow up quickly.

My mother struggled deeply with depression. Because of that, I learned early on that if I wanted to thrive, I would have to depend on myself. I remember my very first day of school. I was six years old, and my mother couldn't take me because she had just undergone surgery. So, I walked to school alone.

I was terrified.

But I did it.

That moment set the tone for the rest of my life.

At school, I faced discrimination. Spanish was my first language—the language spoken in our home—and my Anglo teacher didn't speak it. I struggled to communicate with her and with my classmates. The language barrier made me feel isolated and unseen. Yet over time, I overcame it. I learned English well. Still, the mentality I adopted was this: Born alone. Raised alone. Be alone.

Because of that belief, I didn't allow people to get close to me. And when I did, I often ended up hurt.

I became a survivor of emotional wounds—pain, disbelief, hatred, selfishness, hopelessness. My heart wasn't whole; it was fractured. Like glass with spiderweb cracks running through it.

The Father Who Left

My father failed to provide for me financially and was emotionally absent. He came home only to fulfill his needs as a man with my mother. And when he was done, he would say, "I'll be back tomorrow to take you out."

I always believed him.

He never came back.

He chose another family.

I have a half-sister who was born just one week apart from me—in the same hospital. That's how my mother discovered that my father already had a second family. My parents had been married in Cuba for ten years. My father came to the United States alone, and my mother lived in Spain before eventually coming here.

She begged him to let her return home to be with her parents after hearing rumors that he was with another woman. He lied and told her it wasn't true. When I was two years old, my father walked away. When I was five, he came to my birthday party with my half-sister. I still remember what I was wearing—a red pantsuit. I remember her black hair and dress. I remember the confusion in my heart. I didn't know whether to accept her or hate her.

I was just a child.

But another crack formed in my heart that day.

I watched him choose her over me again and again.

Reflection & Healing

Have you ever felt abandoned by someone who was supposed to protect or love you? What lies did that experience cause you to believe about yourself? How has that pain shaped the way you trust others today? Is there someone you need to forgive, even if they never asked for forgiveness?

Invite God into that memory. What do you sense He wants you to know?

The Lies I Believed

As I grew up, I told myself:

A man will never love me.

I will never get married.

I will never depend on anyone for protection or safety.

My heart became filled with anger and pain from abandonment. I didn't believe that God loved me. For years, I believed lies about my worth—lies rooted in the pain my father caused.

My mother, overwhelmed by depression, loneliness, and betrayal, couldn't show affection either. There were no hugs. No kisses. Just harsh words spoken from a wounded heart. I don't blame her now. But as a child, I interpreted that absence of tenderness as proof that I wasn't lovable.

Divine Protection

Even when I didn't know Him, God knew me.

When I was ten years old, my mother's boyfriend moved into our home. One morning, while I was asleep, he entered my room and began touching my legs. Suddenly, I woke up.

I felt a presence.

I sat up and screamed, "Get out of my room!"

I told my mother what happened. That same day, at knifepoint and with items being thrown around the house, she forced him to leave. He called me a liar, but she believed me.

God protected me.

Years later, I went on a date with a man who suggested we drive around instead of meeting at a restaurant. I felt a nudge in my spirit telling me not to go with him—but I ignored it. He drove me to a forest preserve, parked, and became aggressive. He attempted to rape me. At that moment, I heard God's voice clearly. It's going to be okay.

He gave me the words I needed to de-escalate the situation. My life was in danger, but God was there. The man backed away.

Another time, while driving on icy winter roads, my brakes failed, and my car slid toward a pole. I cried out, "Lord, help me!" My car stopped one inch before impact.

God saved me again.

Healing Begins

In 2001, I accepted Christ as my Savior after being invited to a women's group where I witnessed genuine worship. I was baptized in the name of Jesus, and my life began to change.

Healing took time.

But as my heart softened, I forgave my parents and others who caused me pain throughout my entire life. I began to see them through a different lens—one of compassion instead of resentment. Today, my father tells me, "I don't deserve your forgiveness." I hear the tears in his voice. But I remind him that I love him.

Because I know now that my Heavenly Father loves me.

Psalm 103:2–3 (NIV) says:

"Praise the Lord, my soul, and forget not all his benefits—who forgives all your sins and heals all your diseases."

I experienced that healing firsthand while in the Dominican Republic for a site inspection. The night before my departure, I was in excruciating stomach pain and overwhelmed with anxiety. I feared I wouldn't be able to travel home.

But I called out to God.

As I lay there with my eyes closed, praising Him and asking for healing, I felt His presence. A calm peace washed over me—and the pain disappeared.

My faith made me well.

Reflection & Healing

Is there someone in your life you are struggling to forgive?

What emotions surface when you think about releasing that hurt?

What has unforgiveness cost you emotionally or spiritually?

What would healing look like for you in this situation?

Ask God to help you take one step toward forgiveness today.

The Power of Worship

Darlene Zschech once said, "To be a worshiper is to fall in love with God, the Author of love, and accept the love He has for you." True worship isn't about singing songs—it's about surrendering your heart. Joni Eareckson Tada wrote, "God is especially honored when we offer a sacrifice of praise... words of adoration wrenched from a pain and bruised heart."

When we worship God with our whole hearts, He fills us with His love—and we become conduits of that love to others.

1 John 4:8 reminds us:

"He who does not love does not know God, for God is love."

Robert Coleman said, "True worship can only take place when we agree to God sitting not only on His throne in the center of the universe but on the throne that stands in the center of our heart."

From Religion to Relationship

I grew up surrounded by different religions—Jehovah's Witness teachings from my mother, Santería influences from my father, and Catholicism in my neighborhood.

I was confused.

But when I encountered Jesus personally, everything changed.

Jim May said, "What people need is Jesus Christ, not the Christian religion."

Knowing God personally is what transforms us—not rituals, but relationships.

Treasures in Darkness

Isaiah 45:3 says:

"I will give you the treasures of darkness."

The greatest treasure I found in my darkest moments was God Himself.

He has always been my protector, provider, and Savior—even when I didn't recognize Him. Though I grew up fatherless in the human sense, my Abba Father was always there. And today, I know this truth:

God's love does not fluctuate based on our performance. There is nothing you can do to make Him love you more—or less—than He already does.

People's love may change depending on what we do. God's love never does.

A New Lens

Because of God's healing, I now have compassion for my parents and for those people who have hurt me. I speak life into and love to my mother daily. My strength comes from Jesus Christ.

Without Him, forgiveness would have been impossible.

God designed us to mature in community—where truth and the Holy Spirit work together to shape us into who He is calling us to be.

A pure heart creates clear vision.

A bridled soul knows when to pause, listen, and obey rather than react. The power is in the seed—God's Word—but the outcome depends on the condition of the heart that receives it.

Reflection & Healing

In what areas of your life are you still trying to stay in control?

What are you afraid might happen if you surrender those areas to God?

What would it look like to trust Him with your pain or your future?

How has living in survival mode affected your relationships?

Take a moment to pray and release one burden into God's hands.

Closing Reflection

Today, I am no longer living in survival mode.

I am living in surrender.

I am living in healing.

And I share this story so that believers and non-believers alike may know that no matter how deep the cracks in your heart may be, God is able to mend them with love, joy, peace, patience, kindness, goodness, faithfulness, gentleness, and self-control.

Once you feel God's love—in you, around you, and through you—you will never want to live without it.

Because His love heals.

His love restores.

His love transforms.

And His love never fails.

Reflection

What wound are you carrying?

What is your survival journey?

What light has shone in your life?

About the Author

Maria Elena Ramirez is a faith-driven author, speaker, and travel advisor, she is passionate about helping women find healing, hope, and transformation through God. Her writing journey began during her time at Prayer Ministry School with Elijah House Ministries, where she discovered the power of surrendering pain and embracing restoration.

Inspired by authors like Jessica Sky North and Stormie Omartian, she writes with honesty and compassion to encourage women navigating life's challenges. A proud mother and grandmother, she lives with her family in a close-knit, love-filled home and is dedicated to sharing a message of faith, healing, and renewed purpose.

CHAPTER 9

I Love Me More

Jennifer Sanchez

"God will line up the right people when you are ready for what God has for you."

One Step in the Right Direction

One of the most difficult decisions that I had to make was when I made the choice to walk away from an 18-year marriage. I knew that the relationship was no longer for me when my home life became destructive for my physical well-being. My body started deteriorating, and I was getting rashes and stomach pain. I was getting so forgetful due to the amount of stress I was under that I signed up for therapy to figure out what was wrong with me. Instead of helping me with healing my mind and body, it ended up leading to me ending my marriage. Little did I know the therapist brought so much light to so many unhealthy things. The last thing that I wanted to do was to go through a divorce, but it was inevitable. I was the type of woman who was proud of being a wife, and I loved taking care of my home and husband. Unfortunately, I felt like I was the only one taking care of my home, and everything fell on me. I didn't feel like we were true partners.

My ex-husband and I wanted different things and had different expectations of what we wanted in a marriage. My desire was to be a power couple, and I wanted him to be aligned with that. I knew that marriage was to glorify God, and I wanted to change the world with my husband, except he wanted a stay-at-home wife and to live a simple life. What my ex-husband wanted wasn't a bad thing, but it wasn't what I wanted. I was the woman who always wanted to educate myself, network, and grow. I am highly ambitious and adventurous. I love to challenge myself to be better. During that time, I was already running my coaching business and community, but I was feeling like a hypocrite. I was telling women to pursue their goals and their dreams, yet mine were limited. Many times, I didn't want to upset my ex, so instead of causing a fight, I would suppress my desires. One night, my oldest daughter was having a difficult time as a 14-year-old with her mental health. I knew that was a direct result of all our fights and arguments. I remember lying in bed with my daughter when I found out she was struggling and comforting her. That was the moment I made the decision to end the marriage. I prayed for God to remove my ex-husband from my life. I loved my ex-husband so much that I knew I wouldn't be able to leave on my own. I was with him for so long and I have invested so much in him, it wouldn't be easy to end the relationship, but when you allow God to remove someone from your life, he will make it happen. It can be scary because now you have to accept it. I had to tell myself that I love myself more than him.

His Light Reigns

I knew that I was in God's favor when I made that decision because I felt all the love being removed from my heart for him. I became numb. I have always been anti-divorce and anti-separation, but I also believe that if the man is not honoring you, then he is also being unfaithful. God doesn't want us to be in relationships where we are not being honored. Any earthly father wouldn't like to know how his daughter is being mishandled; why would my heavenly father? There's scripture that says that the husband's prayers will be hindered based on how he treats his wife. According to 1 Peter 3:7, *"Husbands, in the same way be considerate as you live with your wives, and treat them with respect as the weaker partner and as heirs with you of the gracious gift of life, so that nothing will hinder your prayers." A clear command on how a man should treat his wife. I wanted a man to also choose me and want to protect me not only physically but emotionally. I didn't feel safe in that marriage.* I am also a big believer in Proverbs 31. Proverbs 31:10 says, A wife of noble character who can find? She is worth far more than rubies. This is what carried me through all those years I was married, I know that I am more precious than rubies as scripture says, and if a ruby is valuable then I am even more valuable than that. Rubies are a rare gem and some rubies are higher in value than diamonds. Regardless, the marriage was also very instrumental for me to start my women's community and coaching business. I've given birth to three beautiful girls, and planted the seed for my ex to be the man God he has been called to be. The greatest gift that I was able to give my ex was to allow him to find a woman whom he feels is best for him. I remained kind during the entire separation. I was so kind that I helped him pack his things for his new home because at the end of the day he is still my family, and we grew up together. I know that most marriages end terribly and that was not my goal. I wanted to make this as painless as possible for me and my girls. Of course it wasn't all smooth, but I was gracious in the way that I carried myself during that time.

Our Steps are Ordered...Just Walk

God has mysterious ways of aligning you in the right places to find your path and put you towards your destiny. The week my ex-husband left, I attended a real estate conference, and I knew I wanted to be part of that real estate community and learn from them directly. I've seen my friends grow their portfolios and I knew I wanted in. One of my greatest goals was to be a landlord and build passive income so that I can continue to pursue my passion projects without worrying about finances. Since it was right after my ex moved out, I was so desperate to be successful that I had to get in. My vulnerability needed something to focus on. So I borrowed money from my parents to join the real estate community because it wasn't cheap. Signing up for something like this was a big deal for me because I now had to prove to my parents that I can be successful in real estate. I didn't want the money to be used in vain.

Soon after I joined, I began working for the founder of the real estate community, focusing completely on learning the industry. This job became a blessing, providing stability during my divorce when grief sapped my energy for entrepreneurship. I knew that during that season of learning real estate and working with that community I heard God tell me, keep my head down and work. I needed to learn everything that I can from one of the most successful and influential investors in the Midwest. This is something that only God can do, place me in a room with the best. I had God's favor and it showed.

My Ministry Realigned Me

Thank God that my coaching business survived because of my team. I built such a solid team in my women's and coaching community that they knew they needed to step in for me. It was almost as if I created a group for my future self. I didn't know it at the time but my own community saved me from drowning. Grief stripped away my sense of identity. Going from leaving my parents' home at 17 to being with my ex-husband for 18 years, marriage is all I knew. Now I was lost, but I confided in my team, feeling like a fraud after all I'd taught them. I ended up slipping into drinking and distraction, not recognizing myself. Many times, I asked God for help to save me from the addiction and distractions.

He Will Cause You to Shift to Become Realigned

During that season God was quiet, and I couldn't hear from him. I almost lost my faith during that time because I kept falling further and further away. What helped me was finding me. I learned to enjoy my own company and discovered what it meant to feel safe and be myself. This is something I'd never experienced. I focused on figuring out who Jennifer was all while growing as a real estate investor. During the discovery phase, I lost a ton of weight, and I got very focused on my health. I got braces and started working with a personal stylist. I was training for my second marathon and lifting heavy weights. I was taking myself out on dates. I would go to dinners, concerts, theater and events by myself. I was learning to love my own company and my alone time. I was developing and enjoying my friendships that surrounded me.

I remember when I was married, I never had time for myself. The married life was very demanding because so much was expected of me. I had very strict calendars and would beat myself up if I couldn't meet my own deadlines. Moreso, I was worried about getting into arguments because something wasn't met. I didn’t know how to give myself grace. Although, while getting to know myself and discovering who I was, I was able to make mistakes and be ok with messing up. My nervous system started relaxing more and the cortisol started going down. Now the most beautiful experience for me now is to mess up and grow from it and not beat myself up for it. Not only was I learning to be myself, I was also healing my trauma and getting myself out of survival mode. I would go to therapy and seek counsel. Anytime, I felt triggered, I knew I needed to get counseling.

His Goodness is Real

The most amazing thing that I learned out of this entire divorce is not only accepting God‘s goodness for my life, but also recognizing how God put all the key people that I needed in my life during the grieving process for me to heal and overcome.

I got to experience healthy men and specifically be around someone who allowed me to express myself and be vulnerable or angry without any judgment or consequences. That was so healing for me. That was probably the most powerful thing that I received from a male friend. I didn't really have male friendships while married, so even dealing with men was an entirely different experience for me. I didn't know what it meant to feel safe around masculine energy. God gave me some great examples of men that looked out for me and guided me during this time. A lot of these men were in Real Estate, so they mentored me not only in life but in my career. I was in a space where I was getting poured into and I was receiving in all areas of my life. I was learning to live life after divorce. I don't regret getting divorced because I wouldn't be doing all the amazing things that I'm doing now if it weren't for that. I wouldn't have learned how to get into real estate, start building my portfolio, and have multiple rental properties. I wouldn't have been able to get out of huge chunks of debt and build my credit back up. I wouldn't have been able to feel more confident and feel more beautiful.

So many of my friends would tell me that I glowed up. I aged backwards. Now after the season of figuring out who I am. I am now all about expecting and receiving. I've only been a giver and a doer. This time around, I pour in me and continue to focus on me.

I think the healthiest thing that a woman can do is pour into herself. I wanted to be an example for my daughters. I wanted my daughters to see that their mom chose herself. I wanted women in my community to have an example of what can happen when you choose yourself and God. I wanted women to not be afraid to start all over again. I always believed that you better practice what you preach. My integrity is so important in the way that I lead others that I need to be living the life that I am preaching for others to practice. I have the mindset now of receiving and I do not intend on losing it. I worked so hard to be this woman.

I've learned that God never gives his children mediocre, he will only give his best. I am living proof that he was taking care of me the entire time and still does. He has taken me into rooms that I never thought I would step into, he has given me favor with leaders, and I have been blessed with beautiful experiences. Even till this day, I get surprised at how God blesses me. He has brought incredible people into my life that still challenge me whether it's in life, business, or real estate. I have surrounded myself with beautiful people.

Choose His Will...Not Your Own

God wants me to live my fullest potential and be an example for other women so they can truly be happy. I can honestly say even with all the stress from real estate, kids, or work, I am the happiest that I have ever been in my life. I know that this pleases my father in heaven to know that even though I might still have challenges I still trust him fully and I have joy in my heart. We have to be in a receiving mode and feel worthy that we can receive. Believing that you are worthy of receiving and accepting God's favor in your life is what will take you to the levels that your heart desires. God will line up the right people when you are ready for what God has for you. Even though I am sad that my marriage ended, now I am making room for the next marriage to come into my life. Although, this time I am allowing God to bring me his very best.

I have been asked by so many people, "Jen , would you get married again after everything that you have gone through." I say, "absolutely." At the end of the day I value marriage and I know that marriage is an instrument to do God's work. The most beneficial relationship that has helped me grow was my marriage. I believe that my next marriage is still going to help me grow and evolve even more, but this time the person will be part of the assignment God has for my life. In the meantime, I am going to keep living my best life and receive everything God has for me.

Reflection

Which pain has brought you the most growth? How?

How do you want to be perceived by the world?

How are you realizing that things are working out for you?

About The Visionary

Jennifer Sanchez

Jennifer Sanchez is a real estate investor, community builder, media and marketing educator, public speaker, and life and business coach dedicated to helping entrepreneurs turn vision into action. Known for her strategic mindset and results-driven approach, she is passionate about holding individuals accountable to both their personal and professional goals.

Since 2018, Jennifer has empowered hundreds of professional and entrepreneurial women through conferences, retreats, networking experiences, and leadership programs under her organization, WISE (Women's Institute of Self-Development and Efficacy).

Before stepping fully into entrepreneurship, Jennifer built a strong foundation in the nonprofit sector, where she provided financial education, academic advising, and career coaching to thousands of individuals across the Chicagoland area seeking transformative change. She later transitioned into consulting, spending several years as a social media, marketing, and public relations strategist, helping elevate both business and personal brands. Her impact has been recognized by *Negocios Now*, naming her to the Latinos 40 Under 40 Class of 2020.

As a passionate serial entrepreneur, Jennifer remains committed to helping others elevate to their next level of success. You can catch her on *WISE Coffee Chat* on WRMN 1410 AM, as well as on Facebook, LinkedIn, and YouTube, where she interviews restaurant owners, coffee shop owners, and fellow entrepreneurs, highlighting their journeys of growth, resilience, and discovery.

A Simple Prayer of Salvation

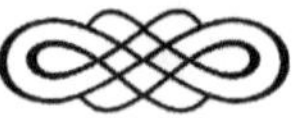

Dear Lord Jesus, I know I am a sinner and ask for Your forgiveness. I believe You died for my sins and rose from the dead. I turn from my sins and invite You to come into my heart and life. I want to trust and follow You as my Lord and Savior. Guide my life and help me to do Your will. Thank You for giving me eternal life and for the new life I now start with You. Be the Lord of my life. In Jesus name, I pray.

Amen.

www.ingramcontent.com/pod-product-compliance
Lightning Source LLC
LaVergne TN
LVHW020647100826
845148LV00012B/2369

* 9 7 9 8 2 1 8 9 4 9 9 9 0 *